A Riddle Flap Book

WHAT'S MY JOB?

By Betty Birney / Illustrated by Lisa Berrett

When a fire starts to burn
I am the one you need.
I jump into my bright red truck
and drive at super speed.

Hocus Pocus, wave the wand
Some think my job is funny.
But no one knows exactly how
My hat can hide a bunny.

A cup of flour, a pinch of salt,
There's so much bread to bake.
And then I spread the frosting,
On your special birthday cake!

A friend to all the animals
Who woof, meow, or baa,
I even tell the hippo
To open and say "aah!"

The rooster wakes me early,
To start my busy day.
I milk the cows and pick the corn
And feed the horses hay.

I dress up in a spacesuit
And soar into the sky.
The earth looks very tiny
From the moon way up so high.